BLUFF YOUR WAY IN ACCOUNTANCY

JOHN COURTIS

Oval Books

Published by Oval Books
335 Kennington Road
London SE11 4QE

Telephone: (0171) 582 7123
Fax: (0171) 582 1022
E-mail: info@ovalbooks.com

First published by Ravette Publishing.
This edition published by Oval Books.

First edition 1987
Reprinted 1990, 1991, 1992
Revised 1993
Reprinted 1994, 1995, 1996
Revised 1997, reprinted 1998
Second edition 1999

Series Editor – Anne Tauté

Cover designer – Jim Wire, Quantum
Printer – Cox & Wyman Ltd

The Bluffer's Guides® series is based
on an original idea by Peter Wolfe.

The Bluffer's Guide®, The Bluffer's
Guides®, Bluffer's®, and Bluff Your
Way® are Registered Trademarks.

CONTENTS

INTRODUCTION

This book is for those who know nothing about accountancy, but feel they ought to; those round the fringes of accountancy who need to know a little more but are deterred by the mystique, and those in accountancy who feel just a little insecure about their grasp of the total picture. This covers quite a lot of people.

There is some confusion about the nature of accountancy. Accountants regard it as a profession. Younger professions regard it respectfully. Older professions (the church, the law and medicine) have accepted it. The oldest profession uses it, professionally.

Dictionaries are more cautious and more likely to define the word as 'the practical art of the accountant'. No wonder that many accountants do feel a little insecure. There are other reasons. John Cleese and others have not just implied but suggested explicitly that accountants are boring. This is not wholly fair and is not adequately supported by impartial and statistically valid research data. For example, even if you accept as a working hypothesis that accountants are boring, it would be most improper to postulate that they are boring because they are accountants.

This is a short book. It would be wrong to make it a formal primer in accountancy. Happily that is not appropriate. It would generate third-degree ennui and leave no space for the more esoteric bits. Also, it is no more necessary to understand accountancy than it is to understand in detail how your calculator and digital watch work. We are not going to turn you into an imitation accountant. Indeed, such a transmogrification might be highly undesirable, if not actionable.

Instead, we offer you a basic grounding which will enable you to mingle with accountants and finance staff without being spurned as a rank outsider. Take comfort from the fact that the most brilliant Finance Director we know is not an accountant, but a Doctor with a background in R&D.

This is why a superficial overview of accountancy and a repertoire of questions relevant to the places where accountancy touches the real world, like reporting, forecasting, client relationships and credit control, will be quite sufficient to convey the impression that you know what the answers should be, and where the slush fund is hidden.

THE FUNDAMENTALS

Book-keeping

It is not necessary to burden yourself with detail about the mechanisms of **book-keeping**. Assume they work and don't meddle with them, like the entrails of your personal computer. However, it is desirable to know some of the words in order that you can change the subject and move to higher things when they crop up.

Book-keeping is almost invariably on the **double-entry** system, but in two layers as well so that in reality there are likely to be three entries for every transaction. Accountants disguise this fact or perhaps do not recognise it because it represents a threat to the concept of double entry.

Prime Entry

The first layer consists of books of prime entry, like **cash book**, **sales day** book, **purchases day book** and **journal** (this last is for all transactions which do not fit easily into the other three types).

All the entries in these, either singly or in total, are then entered twice in the **ledgers**, once on the debit side and once on the credit side.

The Ledgers

The place where the double entry takes place constitutes the second layer.

There are several species of ledger. The **Personal**

Ledger contains the accounts of suppliers and customers, subdivided into **Bought** (or **Purchase**) **Ledger** and **Sales Ledger**. These therefore list the trade creditors and debtors of the business.

The **Nominal Ledger** contains all the impersonal accounts, for abstract things which go to make up the trading and profit and loss account. These include things like sales, purchases, wages, rent, rates, postage and other direct costs and indirect expenses. **Real accounts** mean what they say – nice solid things like major assets, land, buildings and so on. They will also be in the nominal ledger.

A **Private Ledger** is somewhat archaic and is only used by businesses which are so secretive that they want to hide part of the nominal ledger away from the peasants. In this sort of business the employees are the peasants.

It is important to be aware that in most businesses the **cash book** does not record cash in hand. It only records sums in the bank account (unless the business actually trades in cash, as with a retail store). The only cash on the premises is recorded in the **petty cash book**.

Most businesses actively dislike cash these days because it represents a security problem. Those who do like it are generally small traders who like to be able to take money out of the till and feel they are cheating the tax man. You need to be aware that this is an illusion.

If their ratio of profit to turnover drifts below the norm for their type of business the Revenue slaps in an estimated assessment based on the best possible ratios and the poor old hand-in-till shopkeeper has to face the double burden of higher accountants' fees to fight the case and an eventual tax bill higher than his

n inefficient trading genuinely deserved.

You need to know one more thing about small firms' books. If you are about to buy a small cash business, be it pub, shop or restaurant, the present proprietor will always point to two comfort factors.

1. The way business is improving.

2. The fact that the real profits are higher than those shown in the books because he or she has been taking several hundred pounds per week or month out of the cash takings.

Be warned. The most likely scenario is that the business appears to be improving because the former illicit drawings are now being left in the till to create an apparent improvement in the closing months. The true picture is therefore that you are being asked to pay for a non-existent trend and non-existent excess receipts.

Worse, if the business is a limited company and you buy the company, you are liable for the past fiddles when the Revenue eventually catches up. Hire a good accountant.

Double Entry

This simple arithmetical idea is the nub of modern accounting. For every entry on the debit side (generally representing assets, expenses incurred or losses) there must be a numerically identical entry on the credit side of another account (representing liabilities, revenues or shareholders' funds, including profits).

Traditionally, debits are on the left hand side of the

books of account (ledgers) and the credits on the r
hand *except* on a traditional **Balance Sheet**, wh
the reverse applies, to confuse the enemy. All no
accountants are the enemy, by the way.

This system means that if all the entries in the
book are arithmetically correct, not only will they
mean something but the net balances in each account
will, when listed, balance left against right in total.
Quite often, due to human error, they do not. Hence
the need for a **Trial Balance**, which can be done at
any point to check whether the arithmetic is wrong.

This obsession with the possibility of error per-
vades the whole history of accounting and may explain
why the few exams needed for entry to accountancy
training (until recently) included compulsory mathe-
matics.

If you wish to imply massive familiarity with the
process of assembling accounts at a year end, you
must think yourself into the long hours spent poring
over a trial balance which does not balance and know
a few of the reasons why it does not.

Additions, as hinted above, are a classic cause.
More subtle are **transpositions**. All differences divisible by nine probably result from a transposition. For
example, an error of £6300 tells you that someone has
recorded £7000 at one end of the transaction and
£700 at the other.

The same applies with, for example, £879.12 which
to the experienced eye is divisible by 99 and therefore
must be a sum recorded in pounds on one side and
pence on the other – in this case £888.00 and £8.88.
Auditors punch-drunk with fatigue often miss this
and you can look terribly good if you just look at all
such differences for the 9 and 99 factors.

Omissions are another – i.e. a single entry without

a balancing opposite number. Look through the ledgers for the exact amount of the difference. Just one lucky diagnosis of this sort and your reputation is made.

The Uncertainties of Double Entry

Double-entry book-keeping, when properly practised, is a satisfying and self-checking exercise. If the two sides, debit and credit, balance one is normally entitled to expect that the books are arithmetically correct. Alas, this does not mean that they portray a true result. Of the many possible reasons, you need only know two.

The first is that if the data is being processed by a formal accounting software package, the arithmetical truth remains credible.

However, if the data is in the form of a print out from some other program, even a 'spreadsheet', the arithmetical certainty is less certain or altogether absent.

The other problem is that each side of the books has several groups of accounts in it. They are unrelated and differ in principle and effect. For instance, most will include the following types of balance:

Debit (left side)	**Credit** (the right)
* assets	* liabilities
* expenditure	* revenues
* losses	* profits
	* provisions and reserves

It follows logically that if someone inventive can make a loss or an expenditure appear to be an asset, the whole picture will seem better. Similarly, so will the transmogrification of reserves or liabilities into revenues, thus later increasing profits or at least reducing losses.

All these activities are termed creative accounting or fiddling, depending upon your point of view. You need only draw attention to the possible weaknesses. There is no need for proof. That is for the auditors, or the Fraud Squad. But it is important that your audience should appreciate and share your reservations.

The auditors will not mind being advised of such doubts. They are there to sell 'chargeable time' and any excuse for pushing the bill up, within reason, will be welcomed. Until legislation changes, they are watchdogs rather than bloodhounds and do not have an absolute obligation to detect fraud so they won't be too distressed if they seek without finding.

Financial Accounts

Financial accounting is the core of an organisation's total accounting activity. It builds historical data about the financial implications of all activities from the books of prime entry through the ledgers to culminate in the **statutory accounts** as **Balance Sheet** and **Profit and Loss account**.

It records the stewardship activity of the management as distinct from cost accounts and management accounts which exist for control and decision-making purposes. These are optional. Financial accounting is obligatory and if you don't do it properly during the year someone will have to do it after the year end, either for tax or other statutory purposes.

Doing it after the year end, from a brown paper parcel full of vouchers, bank statements, cheque stubs and wages sheets is known as an **incomplete records** exercise, usually performed by accountants in training because their time is cheap, and a lot of effort is going to be wasted in finding the missing documents. There are always documents missing.

Some people, particularly cost accountants, financial analysts and management accountants, feel that financial accounting is very boring. This is not entirely true. Balancing a trial balance or deciding the right place to put the second half of a double entry can be very exciting for the right person. The whoops of joy in the general office when the **TB** balances and coloured pencils are thrown in the air can be quite enervating for onlookers.

Very good financial accountants are allowed to do **consolidations**, which put together several sets of final accounts, often in several currencies. This is the accountancy equivalent of three-dimensional chess, or perhaps draughts. Good consolidations accountants are godlike creatures in their own field. They tend to stay in it.

Cost Accounting

It is important to remember that cost accounting like management accounting, which is a derivative of cost accounting, is optional. It is perfectly possible to run a business without cost accounts and there is no formal legal requirement to have them, although the auditors may look askance at their absence.

It follows that you do not need to know too much

13

about them. You can adopt the posture that the detail of cost accounting is beneath you. Lots of very senior chartered accountants have done so.

It is only necessary to know a few of the key words, and some of the problems.

For example, to a layman, most expenditures are costs. Accountants tend to draw a distinction between **costs**, which belong in the early stages of the production process and can be directly linked to the product (labour, raw materials and so on) and **expenses** which would normally be regarded as overheads, indirectly associated with the product (all the administration staff and high-level conceptual thinkers).

Costs

Accountants like to classify costs so they can be allocated to specific accounts and blamed on specific **cost centres** which are usually discrete departments. A **profit centre** pulls together a number of cost centres and has revenues which permit it to show a profit. A separate company, division, branch or country grouping could be a profit centre.

A useful position is to sneer at any profit centre which does not sell to the outside world. You can be sure that the transfer prices at which it sells products or services to the rest of the organisation cause a lot of internal strife and record fictional or at best disputed profits.

Profit centre managers also waste time trying to get central overhead expense allocated elsewhere.

Expenses

It is necessary to have a position on the classification of expenses and it is not enough to know the difference between **fixed**, **semi-variables** and **variables**. You should know, and be prepared to say, that the classification and later reporting of these expenses is confused because:

a) expenses which should be fixed actually vary;
b) those which are semi-variable vary even more;
c) those which should be wholly variable have a fixed element.

All accountants know these facts to be true, but may be slightly rattled if they learn that the secret has got out. In particular they prefer to suppress the possibility that 'fixed' expenses vary, until it comes as a fresh surprise at the end of each accounting year.

The biggest conceptual problem which accountants face may well be **semi-variable** expenses. If not, the next most likely contender must be total absorption costing. Problems associated with inflation accounting pale into insignificance by comparison, not least because the spectre of inflation sometimes goes away, whereas the other two go on and on.

One of the main reasons why actual expenses frequently differ from budget is the uncertainty of the semi-variable. **Variable** costs, like materials, distribution and sometimes labour, tend to vary directly with the volume of production. **Fixed** expenses, like rent, rates and staff salaries, are fairly predictable.

In between are the dreaded semi-variables, which are often even less predictable than the performance of a recalcitrant steeple-chaser. The problem is compounded by the unwillingness of operational staff to recognise that they vary at all.

Take a very simple example. Manufacturing and distributive companies all wrap or pack products sold. Sometimes the wrapping cost is nil. Sometimes it is negligible. At the other extreme, the cost of the packing can exceed the gross margin on the product sold.

Consider the case of a small but vital fragile spare part going out to a valued customer. It may be so important that a key employee of the customer comes in and places the thing reverently in his sporran, for the ultimate in safe conduct. Packing costs, nil. Alternatively, the despatch clerk, mindful of the customer's importance and the fragility of the part, will pack it lovingly in layers of excelsior, surround it with a purpose-made heavy duty cardboard box and strap it so securely that Houdini would have difficulty getting out. Packing costs? More than the profit on the part, perhaps more than the cost of the part – or its selling price.

The despatch clerk is a very good example of the people who can generate, through pride in their work, semi-variables which take the profit out of such a transaction. They would laugh at any suggestion that they should skimp in these circumstances. The more numerate of them might suggest you should have a minimum order value. The more commercial would suggest you give trivial items away free to generate goodwill *and* save the semi-variable expense involved in accounting for such a transaction. Both would be right. The former are nature's accountants, the latter are nature's marketing people.

Total Absorption

Total absorption costing is of absorbing interest only to a minority of accountants. Some of these are obsessional about its importance. Others are equally convinced of its fundamental flaws. Most accountants regard it as impressive but unnecessary.

The reason it arouses such passions in the cold world of numbers is that in trying to allocate *all* costs and expenses it burdens lots of cost centre and profit centre managers with a wholly arbitrary allocation of expenses which they cannot control and do not recognise as theirs. The accountants' need to defend this wholly indefensible system causes stress on both sides.

Do not get involved in these disputes. Concentrate on **marginal costing** and let expenses which would otherwise be too closely attributed to you get set off against the great grey mass called **contribution** (unless of course your marginal costs are very extreme and you want to draw attention to the net position).

What is Cost?

Every bluffer must be aware that nearly all words in accounting have two or more meanings. Any word unqualified by another is a dangerous over-simplification or a red herring. For example, when someone says 'You can have that at cost', beware.

If you are lucky, they mean **prime cost** which includes only the materials, labour and overhead regarded as directly associated with the unit involved. Note that this is not the same as **variable** or **marginal cost**; which would be even more favourable to you but would cause severe emotional distress to any accountant making such a foolish offer because it could omit some costs which, although fairly allocated to the unit, were not variable.

If you are not lucky, 'cost' is going to mean **fully accounted cost** with an allocation via **total absorption costing** of all the company overheads including the office cat's Whiskas. This semantic euphemism enables accountants to do lots of things 'at cost'.

The Balance Sheet

The Trial Balance mentioned earlier leads inexorably to a **Balance Sheet**, so called because it is a summary of balances at the end of a particular period, grouped into fairly intelligible generic headings and providing a snapshot of the financial state of the organisation at that point. Bluffers should call it a 'snapshot' because this trivialises the thing and distracts attention from its imprecision.

It would be more informative to call the balance sheet a statement of assets and liabilities but the uncertainty about whether it would actually balance, partially but not wholly eliminated by the invention of the trial balance, took precedence over the real meaning of the document during its formative years.

Do not remind accountants of this point. They know only too well that unless the accounts are computerised and therefore arithmetically correct (although potentially meaningless in other respects) the major panics in auditing and accounting are still about getting the books to balance and look meaningful, rather than about taking action as a result.

The people who cobble together the financial numbers are known by old-fashioned titles like **book-keeper** and **financial accountant**, whereas the people who take investigative action will normally be called **management accountants** or **financial analysts**. The latter usually refer to the former as number-crunchers. All those who are more obsessed with the balance sheet than the Profit and Loss Account fall into this category, even analysts in stockbroking firms and in banks. Beware all those who put the balance sheet first.

At this point we regret that you are going to have to learn to read a balance sheet; not perfectly, but well enough for the uncertainty implicit in all balance sheets to cover the rest of your ignorance. This uncertainty is not just the result of the arithmetical worries mentioned earlier. By the time outsiders see a balance sheet it is virtually certain to balance.

The problem now arises from the fact that nearly all the figures on it are in some way philosophically suspect. Knowing how and why they might be wrong is more useful than knowing about high accounting principles. In fact, much debate about high accounting principles relates to **inflation accounting** and ways of presenting **statutory accounts** so as to counteract the effects of inflation. There has been a reduction in this endeavour, because of the temporary lull in inflation but **Current Purchasing Power (CPP)** and **Current Cost Accounting (CCA)** may be heard about again.

As we go through the balance sheet, the defects in each item will be identified.

The Assets

First, if the assets exceed the liabilities, the difference is known as the **shareholders' funds** (or in a small firm, proprietor's funds). If the liabilities exceed the assets there is no net worth, just a deficit, and in theory the organisation should not be trading, although many do, supported by friendly bankers and personal guarantees.

The assets are normally arranged according to the ease with which they can be turned into ready money. Money is the most **liquid asset** – this is easy to remember for anyone who spends it. **Fixed assets**, land and buildings for example, are the least liquid.

On the conventional balance sheet the fixed assets come first, probably to impress the bank manager. They also include things like plant and machinery, vehicles, computers, furniture and things with some degree of permanence.

The uncertainty at this level is that the business is required by statute, accounting conventions and good practice to provide for depreciation over the working life of the asset on a fairly arbitrary basis so that the true value of the assets is clouded. **Depreciation** is the loss in value which an asset suffers from age, or use, or both. Colloquially, it may be used to embrace a provision for that loss. The uncertainty factor can best be understood if you compare:

a) freehold land, which is likely to be appreciating in monetary terms, with
b) the buildings on it, which may be either appreciating or wearing out, but will have to be depreciated, and
c) the more fragile assets like computers and motor vehicles which lose a substantial chunk of their value the day they are brought into use.

This is why accountants are always searching for the philosopher's stone marked 'inflation accounting' in the hope that it will solve half of the problem.

Current assets are easier. There are three groups:

1. That which includes stock and work in progress (the least marketable). American companies call stock 'inventory'. So do trendy British ones. Your preferred position, as the person who asks the right questions, is to ask about the split between raw materials, work in progress and finished products. These last are relatively liquid. Work in progress may take days or months to filter through the process. Raw materials take longer. For example, there is a pile of pig iron on the Dagenham marshland. The bottom pigs were there when Henry Ford was alive and were still there 20 years later. Not very liquid.

2. That which includes things like investments (marketable and otherwise), debtors (i.e. customers' accounts) and prepayments (rent paid in advance, for instance). The uncertainty factor primarily affects the unquoted investments, whose valuation can afford some scope for **creative** or **conservative** accounting. Cynics would also enquire about the nature of the provision (overprovision or under) for bad debts, another key area of uncertainty.

3. That which includes very liquid assets, such as:
   — cash on deposit
   — cash at bank, on current account
   — cash in hand

There is relatively little uncertainty here, except that, as with the previous group, in times of inflation the real worth of cash and debtors may be going down. At least with stock you can raise the price by the time it is sold. No such protection applies with money.

One other asset may appear on a few balance sheets. It is known as **goodwill**. It usually arises when a company purchases another business for more money than the net assets (assets less liabilities) involved. Traditionally, this excess cost was regarded as the 'goodwill' of the business and treated as an intangible asset, in other words capitalised on the asset side of the balance sheet.

This treatment is nowadays regarded as creative but unhelpful, so goodwill tends to be written off, i.e. to vanish by being offset against a slice of the reserves which form part of the shareholders' funds. You are entitled to raise an eyebrow sceptically at any recent balance sheet which contains a substantial sum for goodwill. You could legitimately say that the profits of the business are supposed to prove the existence of goodwill. A spurious figure among the assets does not. Any balance sheet which includes an insubstantial sum for goodwill is also suspect. They must be desperately padding or totally devoid of reserves against which to absorb the goodwill.

Accountants have another word for the more liquid current assets. They are known as 'quick assets' because they can be realised fairly promptly. Debtors fall in this category (although it may be a struggle to make them truly quick); cash does; stock does not.

All these assets total one side of the balance sheet. Do not be overly impressed by the gross total. The true worth of the company is represented by the difference between assets and liabilities. Huge totals on both sides and a small net difference offer more chance of incorrect valuation than the same difference between smaller totals each side.

The Liabilities

The second half of the balance sheet includes **liabilities** and **proprietors' funds**. In a conventional balance sheet it is the left hand side. As with the assets, it is arranged in ascending order of liquidity. In other words, it starts with the things you cannot get out easily, or at all in most cases; i.e. the proprietors' funds (share capital in a normal company). It can only be realised on the closure or certain types of sale of the business, and on closure there is seldom enough to pay back the shareholders.

The rest of the proprietors' funds will consist of retained profits and sometimes a **share premium account**, which arises when shareholders pay the company more than the nominal value of its shares to acquire them. All reserves are retained profits of some kind.

The next category, **long term liabilities**, starts with **loan capital**, which pays interest to the investor and will normally have to be repaid eventually at a specified time or within a specified span, so that the company can decide whether it is best to redeem at the beginning or the end.

Long term loans, perhaps secured on mortgage, come next, followed by **deferred liabilities** (like future tax arising from past profits).

In theory, all the above constitute the business's fixed and loan capital. However, modern accountants have brought to a fine art the technique of using the next item, **creditors' accounts** (otherwise known as **payables**) as an essential part of the working capital of the business. They do not like having attention drawn to this. But look carefully at the balance sheet where the official capital appears small in relation to the turnover. You will almost certainly note that sleight of hand is maintaining disproportionately large creditor figures. Look for the ratio.

If the spread between annual purchases and creditors is narrower than, say, 10:1 in a business sector where normal terms are 30 days, the creditors are being used as a source of finance. In some retail businesses which sell for cash but creditors are on 14 or 30 days' credit (with double that period actually taken), the creditors may vastly exceed the stock and debtors, so that the business needs virtually no cash resources to run. It is important to be aware of this because if you are supplying a business like this, there will be no current assets for the creditors when they go bust.

Worse, the ease with which one can start trading in these sectors tempts the very people who are prepared to go bust at the drop of a hat.

It is not necessary to memorise all the ratios which analysts use in comparing balance sheets. One will do. It is the **quick ratio**, that between quick assets (see above) and current liabilities. If the latter (excluding an agreed overdraft) exceed the former, there must be some doubt about the solvency of the business.

If you choose to have dealings with such a business, be firm about your credit control. Bad debts, before they became bad, were doubtful; and before that they were overdue (because of someone's inadequate credit control). Be warned. This sort of business will always be prepared to pay a determined creditor in preference to a weak one, particularly if the determined creditor's armoury includes the threat of liquidation.

Strangely, the really professional late payers are not offended by firm tactics. They regard the juggling act as a game and actually admire good technique.

One masterly financial director of a distinguished but insolvent television company spent a year fending off creditors and only paying against the documentation which would have had the company wound up. Even writs were a licence to delay. One creditor complained that the accounts payable system was not working, only to be advised that it was working perfectly, but its objectives were somewhat different from the norm.

The Profit and Loss Account

If you have any difficulty with the balance sheet, we have good news and bad news. The bad news is that the balance sheet is relatively simple, in that it is a record of the financial position of a business at a point in time and the facts are ascertainable. The good news is that, although the profit and loss account is less certain in its content, the experts get confused too.

Do not be afraid of the **balance sheet audit** which concentrates on verifying the picture. What accountants tend not to tell others is that when the affairs of a business are hopelessly confused the accountants do two balance sheet audits – one at the beginning of the period and one at the end. The difference in net worth is of course the profit (or loss) for the period. All the complex data in the **P & L a/c** boils down to this simple fact. If the net worth of the business has increased in the period, there is a profit. A decrease means a loss. All the accounting flim-flam in the world cannot conceal this if the balance sheets are true and prepared on the same basis.

The problem is that although the change is ascertainable, the way it happens is complex, and can also be affected by decisions to provide for expenses not paid at the end of the period. Provisions for doubtful debt, for instance, or for the results of lawsuits. Here are the main uncertainties and other confusions which afflict the users.

Normally you will only see the detail of the trading account if you are working in the business. In published accounts, the statutory ones, all you are likely to see is a very crude statement of turnover (excluding VAT) less cost of sales, leading to a gross profit figure from which the overheads are deducted, with a few specifically stated because the Companies Act or current accounting practice so requires. This brief treatment masks a hotbed of material which causes major trauma within the company.

Everyone usually agrees that the 'cost of sales' figure is necessary because it includes only direct costs and expenses clearly necessary to the generation and sale of the product or service.

You can't sell an omelette without buying some eggs (unless you own chickens, which would be known as **vertical integration** and is quite beyond our present brief) so everyone accepts the cost of the eggs as 'direct'. It is the downward progression, from the gross profit at the end of the trading account to the final pre-tax figure, which causes most internecine strife within companies.

26

Most trading accounts show a profit. You have to be fairly dim or very unlucky to give away products or services so cheaply that the trading account shows a loss. However, the body of the profit and loss account deducts from this gross profit all the expenses which the production people regard as luxuries rather than essentials. For the production staff, the ideal world is one where the customers come to the factory gate, buy what the factory happened to make that day, pay in cash and come back the next day for more.

Unless you are running a stall selling free range eggs at the farm gate this dream is seldom realised. There are nuisances like accountants, directors, sales staff, marketing staff, personnel staff, buildings to house them in, advertising expenses, distribution costs, bank charges, audit fees, legal fees and security guards. All these at certain times can seem like non-essentials. Even depreciation can seem unreal.

Equally, people in charge of the various cost centres which bear these costs fight bitterly over accepting fringe items into their particular slice of the accounts. Be aware that these problems exist but stand aloof from them. What you are interested in is the well known **bottom line** of the profit and loss account. Concentrate on this because, as far as anything is certain, this is coming close to the certainty of the difference between the opening and closing balance sheets. The only variation will arise from what are known as **below the line** items.

Once upon a time creative accounting could shift many things below the line so that a massive profit was reduced by **extraordinary items** which directors barely acknowledged as happening in the same country let alone in their/your company. The rules have tightened, and anything below the line is there because it satisfies strict statutory requirements. Or 'best practice' rules from the accounting bodies.

Generally they should be very unusual one-off items or perhaps capital profits or losses of a unique nature. Cast a cynical eye at them but be less suspicious than you would have been two decades ago.

The other sleight-of-hand to watch for is any statement about changes in accounting practices. As a general rule, all such changes distort the net profit in some way in the period concerned. Take a friendly accountant into a corner and ask for the effect to be explained. This has two advantages. It will increase your knowledge of the business and the games the directors are playing. It will also flatter the accountant concerned. For maximum results the accountant should also be of the opposite sex.

Note also that the provision for taxation is almost invariably a conservative one. No auditor is going to sign a set of accounts which understates the possible tax burden arising, but they will all quite gaily sign against the maximum provision, and then let their tax departments work like hell to avoid paying that figure. Only if they and the company get their sums or their principles wrong will the full amount, or any greater one, be paid.

In the final analysis, see if the net profit is better than last year, by an amount more than sufficient to offset inflation and if not, keep asking why, very firmly.

You also need to know, although it is seldom described thus on published accounts, that the final bit of a Profit and Loss Account is formally known as the **Profit and Loss Appropriation Account**, because this is where the hard earned monies are passed out to shareholders and various bottomless pits. It is not considered funny to refer to it as the Misappropriation Account, however much your later researches lead you to that conclusion.

It is at this level in the accounts that **dividends** to shareholders appear. So do transfers to various high-sounding reserves. In the great days when the Companies Act actually permitted banks to establish unlimited secret reserves they sometimes, not always, went this route.

Beware the transfers to **reserves**. Stuffing excesses into the pension fund is no longer considered legitimate but it is important to remember that a reserve is only a reserve because it lacks the certainty which would qualify it as a provision.

You can rest assured that if any reserve could be turned into a provision it would, because of the tax effects. Most provisions are allowable for tax. At this stage it may be helpful to consider why proprietors seek to manipulate the accounts.

First, why do people want to improve the balance sheet?

a) To impress bankers, suppliers and creditors with an illusion of greater solvency.
b) Because it is an automatic by-product of improvements to the profit figures.

Second, why bother to worsen the balance sheet?

a) Usually as a by-product of the conservative accounting necessary to lower profit figures (see below), or
b) To facilitate a management buy-out at a depressed price.

Third, why improve the profit figures in the P & L a/c?

a) To protect the directors' reputations or bonuses.
b) To assist a sale at a firm price.
c) To deter a bid at the wrong price.
d) To cover fraud.

Fourth, why worsen the profit figures?

a) To minimise the tax bill.
b) To hide profits from non-director shareholders.
c) To hide profits from the unions.
d) To hide excess profits from customers, particularly governments, who take a particularly dim view of this, whether or not cost-plus contracts are involved.

Given all these reasons, which can seem very compelling to the people involved, it is not surprising that from time to time a large example of creative or conservative accounting slips past even the best auditors.

Another trade secret about auditors is that they are not too worried about conservative accounting. Anything the directors do which makes it likely that the net worth of the company is understated gives them great comfort. They know to their own and their insurers' cost that accountants generally get sued when the assets are deficient, not when they are in surplus. Unless they suspect you are engaged in a massive tax evasion exercise anything less is tolerable, particularly if debated on a high moral plane beforehand.

There is another reason for this. Auditors usually have little confidence in the audit process and suspect there may well be an unintentional over-valuation elsewhere, even when the directors are busy undervaluing stock, debtors and anything else in sight. The known undervaluation reduces the chances that the unknown will sneak up on them later.

Other known reasons why there could always be trouble ahead include:

- The reduction over the last three decades in Chartered Accountants' work/training experience from five years to four, to three, and now two and a bit.

- The assumption that computerised accounts must be right. You know that this is a fiction for two reasons. First, balancing numerically does not prove the accounts tell the truth. Second, computerised accounts only balance on paper if programmed to do so. Fraud, incompetence and bugs can all prevent this.

- The extraordinary scale of modern business and thus the potential for honest error, to say nothing of the other kind.

- The fact that many PCs and even some big ones with expensive programs are not equipped to cope with the year 2000, so will crash or otherwise react adversely to the first entry for that period.

- Accountants' liking for computer games tempts them to stuff into their machines any new free game received on disk, regardless of the risk of computer viruses accidentally or deliberately co-existing with it – something which is causing rather more concern than the millennium bug.

THE FANCY BITS

Management Accounting

You may feel that management accounting implies accounting for management. There is some misunderstanding on this point.

What managers say they want from accountants is 'information'. This is a code word meaning (depending on the managers and the circumstances): solutions, ratio analyses, ideas, decisions, good news, recommendations, panaceas, excuses, culprits, therapy, whitewash or moral support.

The misunderstanding arises because few managers tell their accountants that the word is in code. Fewer tell them which code is in use this week. In consequence, if they are lucky, they may get information. If they are not lucky they just get plain old-fashioned accounts, which to the average accountant are management information at its best.

Management accounts are an accountant's view of what management wants. Unless they are received and improved by strong non-financial managers, they may be useless, or worse.

Given that you are operating in a less than perfect environment, you are not likely to change the world overnight, so the art of the possible dictates that you find a way to interpret what is available, rather than amend or replace it.

Start with the assumption that the existing management accounts are wrong. This is invariably true in any business big enough to need them. However, never say they are wrong, just in case you cannot prove it, or the management accountants (analysts) are too political to admit it. Instead, say that you are "unhappy" with the period's figures and ask questions that highlight areas in which non-accountants can share your doubts, even if they are not on your side.

It is acceptable, and may come as a revealed truth, to point out that in most businesses most variances tend to be unfavourable. This is because people outside and inside the business are much more likely to generate accidental costs and expenses than to find 'windfall' revenues. The prime characteristic of a windfall, as Sir Isaac Newton found, is that it raps you smartly on the occiput and, unless you want to discover gravity, this comes as an unpleasant surprise.

It follows that reporting against budgets will throw up some of these variances (which lead you to exceed the expense budget) and omit some (which come as a nasty shock later when the financial accounts are compared with the management accounts).

Integrated Accounts

It is often alleged by an organisation's accountants that the management accounts are wholly integrated with and derived from the financial accounts. This is another myth.

One of the main reasons why accountants in commerce and industry go into a deep depression just before and just after the end of the financial year is that this is the time when the chickens come home to roost and it becomes apparent even to the meanest intellect that there is a yawning gulf between the real figures (the books of account, which lead via the financial accounts to the annual statutory report) and the figures on which management has been relying for the past 11 months, so that the generally favourable impression these have created is totally erroneous.

Now we come to the trade secrets: the reasons why all accountants know the figures are likely to be wrong, although this realisation retreats readily to their subconscious mind and appears to come to them quite fresh whenever in the accounting period the facts emerge.

It is vital to have the ear and the respect of the analysts. Happily, most of them have an Achilles heel which, with a little effort, can remind them that they have feet of clay, but still keep the fact secret from everyone else. The magic formula is to ask for their help in one specific area of analysis. Go to them after a month in which the organisation has done particularly well according to the preliminary figures and ask, nay insist, that they investigate the reasons for the favourable variances. This will usually come as a surprise to them.

The average investigative team is likely to be sitting on its collective butt breathing a quiet sigh of relief and waiting for the next crisis. They will want to know why you are interested. It is permissible to tell them, because when you are proved right (this is a win/win deal – you will always be right) you will look omniscient. The fact that you have come to them quietly with the news is going to earn you respect and kudos.

There are three things to investigate:

1. The first is the possibility that too much revenue has sneaked into the period's accounts. This is usually a

34

calendarisation error which means the sum involved should have been in the previous period – or the next one.

2. The second is the equally strong possibility that a significant chunk of costs or expenses has been omitted. Again, it will be in the wrong period, previous or subsequent, unless there is a backlog in the accounts-payable function and someone's desk drawer is stuffed with unprocessed invoices from suppliers. Fortunately this cannot happen at the revenue end, unless someone on a profit-related bonus has noticed that this period is crucial for bonus purposes and has massaged the revenue figures (difficult, often fraudulent, but not impossible).

3. The third is a more worthy cause. You want to know the real reason why it was such a good month, so that the organisation may be equipped and motivated to repeat the effort. (This always wins.)

Points (1) and (2) will not astound the analysts, although they will kick themselves if they had not thought of them first. The third will often do so. Analysts spend so much time analysing that they have little or no time to go out and influence management to do something with the figures. The idea that they might venture forth with good news, demanding a repeat performance, is likely to strike them as so radical that they prefer to delegate upwards or sideways – to the Controller, or even to you.

Analysts never forget that in olden days the messenger who brought bad news frequently lost his head. The principle still applies, aggravated by the fact that this sort of company has senior managers who cannot tell good news from bad unless it is colour-coded or explained to them very slowly and in words of one syllable.

You must remember that nearly all the things noted above which could cause favourable variances can happen in reverse and generate unfavourable ones. It is not necessary to list all the variances in the accountant's knapsack but a gentle catalogue of questions exploring the possibilities can be guaranteed to unsettle both accountants and managers whose areas are in the spotlight, for two reasons:

1. The first is the possibility that you could by accident be right.

2. The second is that you obviously know the questions to ask and therefore may know something about the underlying facts that they don't know.

Some of the questions derive from the errors listed above. Others could include:

a) Checking the additions, so you can ask about the anomalies which result.

b) If any report descends into a morass of numbers, asking what they mean in plain words, and keep on asking.

c) Checking the dates. A surprising number of documents do not bear dates. Busy accountants occasionally issue last month's figures if they are putting together a package at midnight. Everybody will be grateful if you save them from asking fatuous questions about a wholly irrelevant set of figures.

d) In a multi-company environment asking which company or divisional grouping is covered if this is not clearly specified – for the same reason.

e) In a review meeting, asking the presenter to review the highlights. This buys time and may also achieve explicit disclosures not evident, or present, in the text.

f) Checking by enquiry, mental arithmetic or calculator, whether the key ratios are the same as for the previous period. Asking diffidently about the ones that are not, as if the matter may be beneath them and you.

g) Asking the presenter if he or she has any indication of different trends since the period covered by the report. This is for two reasons. First it is not unknown for a group of articulate senior managers to sit in uncomplaining silence, even though each knows that recent events have made the paperwork obsolete, because each has a very good reason for keeping quiet. Second, it gives you the chance to venture into territory unsupported by text or hard fact, where your questions sound doubly credible because there are no facts to discredit them.

h) Asking the presenter what conclusions you are supposed to draw. This is not as naïve as it sounds. Put blandly it can sound very professional, not least because most accountants will have omitted to provide a summary or recommendation and will hate you for this.

All's fair in love, war and profit reporting.

Budgets

A **budget** is an annual plan of the financial progress of a business. It is important that you are fluent in the vocabulary of budgeting and are aware how imperfect budgets can be, and why. This largely relieves you of the obligation to take them seriously. It will also reduce the risk that you will be asked to compile them. Very few managers, financial and other, are likely to entrust the articles of their faith to a known atheist. You do not invite a pacifist to play cowboys and indians.

Budgets come in several forms. The most common one and the one most likely to be called just 'the budget' is actually a **profit budget**. It covers the predicted content of the trading and profit and loss accounts. Others include:

- The **current asset budget**, which derives from the former and leads to a cash flow forecast for the period.

- A **capital budget**, which concentrates on the non-revenue items and also provides input to the cash flow calculations.

- A **headcount** (or manpower) **budget** which is not expressed in financial terms but connects vaguely to the forecast 'people-costs' in the primary budget.

Do not be overawed by budgets. There are so many ways of presenting them, and compiling them, that they look complex and authoritative. They are not.

Some accountants claim that **zero-based budgets** avoid traditional budget errors. This is true. Unfortunately they introduce new ones. A zero-based budget starts with a clean sheet of paper and builds up the numbers with a total disregard for what has gone before. This allegedly ensures that you do not slavishly reproduce last year's errors. It also ensures that you forget to include large but infrequent expenses. The managers of the areas concerned are not always helpful. They, like you, want to be in a position to cast doubt on the budgets before long.

Best estimates and/or extrapolations from last year's actuals are better bases in this context.

The key reason you can always sneer at budgets, even if you were a party to them, is that most accountants tend to generate budget information (with or without input from operational managers) and then fail to obtain agreement from the management team for the full budget package which results. In consequence even the least numerate 'broad brush' manager who could look at the totals and know instinctively that they are rubbish, does not have the chance to do so before the year is well under way, by which time it is better to keep quiet. They can blame the budget development process later, when actual results look sick.

The ugly truth is that **the actuals** always prove the budgets wrong. (Always call the actual results 'the actuals'.) The massive authority generated by the sophisticated compilation process is eroded as soon as the first few months of the year have passed and flaws are visible. It is at this point that managers suddenly become numerate and point knowingly to all the weaknesses they kept quiet about in the first place. They know, better than most accountants, that budgets can never be perfect. Unlike most accountants, they have no professional belief in their innate rightness. This gives them a clearer view.

Budgets go wrong in three ways:

1. The revenues are exaggerated because nobody wants to be a prophet of doom at the beginning of the year. Sales people in particular regard budgets merely as targets to be aimed for, rather than best estimates of likely performance.

2. The costs are underestimated for similar emotional reasons and because it is easy to forget the occasional, the non-standard, the windfalls and the cost inflation which cannot be passed on in pricing action at the other end.

3. The calendarisation is wrong, i.e. straight line, when it should be seasonally adjusted, or vice versa. Either can create a fool's paradise halfway through the year.

Creative Accounting

Creative accounting is a twilight area. In the tax field there is a clear distinction between evasion, which is illegal, and avoidance, which is legal and respectable. The position about creative accounting is unclear. Most textbooks do not mention it. There is no formal definition. It is a discreet process of manipulating things like pension funds, tax provisions, fixed assets, stock and reserves or other specific provisions, so as to improve the apparent net worth of the company and/or its profits.

Those who do it will always defend it as a legitimate exercise within the bounds of accounting conventions. You will note that they only defend it when it is discovered. They do not mention that creative accounting is under way, until found out.

The opposite of creative accounting is **conservative accounting** which involves pliancy in the other direction. Auditors are more sympathetic to it, because they don't normally get sued when the assets exceed the reported total.

You are allowed to be ambivalent about creative accounting, indeed this is the preferred posture. Being wholly in favour of it would imply an eagerness to walk the tightrope, or plank. Being wholly against it suggests a degree of conservatism bordering on the reactionary.

If you have to take a firm stand on specifics we advise mild approval for:

a) anything acceptable to the auditors, like shifting certain costs 'below the line'

b) flattering fixed asset and stock values

c) taking the most 'realistic' view of tax provisions.

But frown on any tampering with facts or pension funds and points which actually have to be hidden from the auditors rather than debated or explained to them.

You could also express semantic reservations about the description 'creative' accounting for anything which reduces profits and, inexorably, net assets, because this is merely a pursuance of good old fashioned conservative accounting – which would be creative if it were more devious.

Social Accounting

Accountancy is not just a profession, or a practical art. The cheering fact is that accountancy is primarily about rendering everything into monetary terms, whether the exercise makes sense or not. The process makes things more intelligible to accountants and generally less intelligible to everyone else.

The most extreme example of this professional lunacy is the ill-fated concept of human asset accounting, later known as **human resource accounting**, which attempts to attribute a monetary value to all the money spent on the training and development of employees, with a blatant disregard for the fact that no legal system in the civilised world attributes any degree of ownership or even medium-term rights in people to their employers.

Even in the production process accountancy transforms units, which can be anything from books to battleships, into monetary terms. This ensures that the accountants feel comfortable although the operational staff immediately lose their grasp of the proceedings.

You will recall that in primary school you were taught not to add apples and pears. Seven apples and fourteen pears were not to be artificially lumped together. It appears that accountants did not learn this lesson. They were probably out in the playground falsifying the attendance records or the milk roster.

Beware the seductive and spurious precision of the accountant's art. Any document is flawed which contains the solid certainty of freehold land (probably undervalued), cash (correctly valued but wasting away under inflationary pressures) and the uncertainty of deferred tax (whose precise amount and whose eventual appearance as a liability are both suspect).

This knowledge should enable you to feel perfectly at ease in the presence of accountants.

If you really want to rattle an accountant in industry or commerce, or unnerve a chairman at an annual general meeting, **human liability accounting** is a possible tool.

Human liability accounting is the opposite of human asset accounting and it poses the much more interesting concept that employing people is a monumental nuisance and potentially very expensive. The following key questions are virtually unanswerable, but ought not to be:

- "What is our total contingent liability in respect of redundancy payments if we were to dismiss the complete workforce?"

- "Why is it not shown on the balance sheet?"

- "How many employees with access to the computer are not bonded (insured and checked against fraudulent action)?"

- "Are we insured against the costs of female employees of child bearing age taking maternity leave at our expense?"

- "If they all did it at the same time, what is the total contingent liability involved? (Not too theoretical – remember what happened to the birthrate nine months after the great North American blackout.)"

You can probably devise some more of your own,

given local knowledge, but these should be enough to remind everyone of the risks. If not, try the wider concept: "How many employees with access to specialist product or market knowledge do not have a restraint clause in their contracts of employment, or have no contract of employment?"

We guarantee there is no company which has a clear conscience on all the above.

A contributor to the insecurity factor is that accountancy is very simple conceptually. This is the trade secret. There is no mystique. Remember that the high point of accountancy is double-entry bookkeeping, whose unique merit is that the debits are balanced by credits in other accounts; not the same ones, or the limited intellectual challenge would have vanished altogether, unless of course the second half of the transaction is cunningly disguised as something else.

It is correct to compare double-entry book-keeping to Newton's Third Law of Motion: 'To every action there is an equal and opposite reaction.' This makes you look erudite and also reminds any accountants within earshot that there is a real world outside.

Finally, just to get everything fully in proportion, bear in mind that the bread and butter of the accountancy profession is the **statutory audit**. Audits are like funerals. They are needed but nobody actually wants them, except the accountants and the undertakers.

Armed with this knowledge you can feel secure about infiltrating or fighting the accountancy mafia who are already feeling insecure because fewer companies and partnerships now need a statutory audit – an interference which upsets the public practice accountants' god-given right to fees from everyone.

44

ACCOUNTANTS

Members in Practice

The accountancy profession refers to the people who stay behind in the public practice firms (rather like schoolboys who go back to the old school as masters as soon as they've finished at university) as 'members in practice'.

They come in all shapes and sizes – the firms, that is, not the people – but there are four basic groups:

1. The smallest is the **sole practitioner**, a breed of which the Institutes quietly disapprove because, when they fall ill, there is no backup. So they tend to damage the reputation of the profession as a whole. They will either be specialists at a high level, in tax perhaps, or generalists at a very low level with undemanding clients.

2. The **small firm**, with two to five partners, probably generalist but with no major clients.

3. The **medium-sized firms**, with 6 to 20 partners. These used to be the mainstay of the profession. Big enough to be competent all-rounders but still of a size to be intimate and with a clear identity. Alas, many of them have felt the urge to merge and have been swallowed by one of the majors or joined with another firm of similar size and usually achieved the worst of both worlds.

4. The **majors**, whether you call them the big five/six, top 12 or top 20, are huge, and usually international by formal or loose associations. If you are uncertain where a particular firm lies in the ranking, note carefully how they describe the top end of the

profession, and their position:

- 'Probably the largest' means they are number two
- 'In the big eight' means they are eighth or seventh
- 'In the top 24' means 21 through 24.

Although we do not advise turning yourself into a replica of a qualified accountant, because it is socially unacceptable in some circumstances and actionable in others, there may be occasions when you wish to convey the faint impression that you have had some relevant training at some time in the past.

For this you can choose the body most relevant to your past or change your past to fit the qualification.

Accountancy Services

Most professions have a love/hate relationship with their clients. Accountancy is no exception, except that clients are compelled by law to use accountants and are therefore even less sympathetic than they might be in a free market.

The climate varies directly with the financial results. If the accountants save or make money for the clients, all is well. If they merely cost money the atmosphere is neutral. If they lose money or are perceived as too expensive, the relationship deteriorates rapidly.

It is necessary to examine the services which the profession provides to clients to understand where these problems can arise. They fall into five main categories.

1. The core product is **the audit**. Nearly all audits

are done because statute or custom demands. Hardly any are at the victims' choice but few cause problems.

2. **Book-keeping** and **accountancy** services come next, often hand in hand with the obligatory audit. Again, few create disaster.

3. **Tax work** follows inexorably. This is the problem area. People and companies hate paying tax. They also hate accountants who fail to prevent such payments. This is often because they fail to recognise the difference between compliance and planning.

Compliance is the business of computing and negotiating tax liabilities after the event. This is the area where most clients expect accountants to have a dramatic impact. They often do, but the impact is frequently a nasty shock, as the upright accountant has to point out that the tax consequences of the 'event' are highly unfavourable and, without fraudulent retrospective manipulation, cannot be improved. This is why, for those with foresight, tax planning is so popular and, for those without foresight, visionary accountants are in demand.

Tax planning is usually regarded as a formal process of consultation before the event, or the tax year, or the accounting year. In practice, it is a hectic and continuing process during which the accountants (in-house and external) desperately try to find out if a taxable event is about to happen so that they may:

- prevent it
- diminish it
- time it properly
- structure it properly
- move it offshore

47

- make it a non-event for tax purposes or
- complement it with an event attracting tax relief.

The all-time great tax planners are not those who invent complex schemes, sailing closer to the wind than an Olympic dinghy helmsman. These schemers tend to spend a lot of time arguing precedents in court and also have their homes, offices, dustbins and mistresses raided by crack teams of Revenue investigators in combat gear. Instead, the greats beaver away quietly, deferring, offsetting and minimising the tax profile of the chargeable events and moving them into a lower tax bracket.

This earns no OBEs but it avoids jail and makes the clients quite happy. It also prevents the Revenue flagging the clients' records for special attention next year.

4. **Insolvency**. Insolvency departments aid and administer companies before and after they discover they are broke (or someone else discovers it). It is important, and will make you very popular, to be able to point out that insolvency departments save more companies than they terminate.

5. **Systems**. Systems departments can make the same claim, but the method is different. The outsider's assumption is that they do this by installing new computers and software. In practice, it is vital to be aware that the solutions are more varied, including:

— avoiding computers by improving manual systems
— making the existing computer work better
— helping you sue the people who put it in.

Systems departments can be as unpopular as tax departments because they are held responsible, rightly or wrongly, for things (omissions or commissions) which cost money and cause distress. They can also be blamed for the sins of hardware and software suppliers.

In all circumstances never forget you have the option to counter any question with "What sort of figure had you in mind?"

Clients

There is a curious role reversal from one end of the client scale to the other. Accountants' clients range from real individual people with tax problems, at the lower end, to major corporations at the other. The small client, whether individual or 'sole trader' is relatively dependent on the accountant and indeed the practice management courses of various institutes invariably turn to ways the accountants can get rid of the smallest clients or charge them more.

At the other end of the scale, the major audit practices, although firm with their clients, are nonetheless dependent and deeply regret losing the fees associated with a major audit.

Accountants regard **Architects** as clients, but not exciting ones. Architects regard accountants in practice as a necessary evil and, as potential employees, unnecessary. However, neither side manages to generate the profound contempt which characterises relations with some other professions.

The Armed Services: accountancy does not play a large part in the work of the armed services and, apart from a slight bulge in numbers during and just after National Service, there is no place for qualified accountants in the military. This is remarkably like the Treasury which was at one time virtually devoid of accountants. It now borrows them at high level because of the impossibility of attracting them to a career there.

The Church: a few accountants work for the major churches and a few accountants become priests, vicars and preachers but the two professions have little to say to each other. Men of God feel that accountants worship Mammon and accountants feel that men of God always want little audits and accounts done cheaply or free without realising how much professional indemnity insurance costs these days. There is no meeting of the minds.

Estate agents: accountants do not recognise estate agents as belonging to a profession. They recognise chartered surveyors of course, but as so many of these work as estate agents there is a gulf.

Medicine: accountants hate doctors because they always expect miracles in tax avoidance after the event and yet never keep enough vouchers to achieve even fair play on the events concerned.

Solicitors: accountants have a love-hate relationship with the law. On the one hand they wish the legal profession were unnecessary and also suspect solicitors of stealing certain aspects of their advisory work (the feeling is mutual) and on the other, they recognise the need for a second opinion from time to time. It is also very reassuring to have taken counsel's opinion when things go wrong.

Banking: there is some suggestion that banking is a profession. This is probably spread by those merchant bankers who are not members of some other profession (like accountancy and the law) or clearing bankers with ideas above their station.

Whatever the case, accountants tolerate and grudgingly respect merchant bankers to the extent that major accountancy firms have in several cases set up departments which purport to offer much of the advice which a merchant bank would offer. The effect is slightly weakened by their inability to offer a wide enough range of banking services, like money.

Similarly, accountants and solicitors hold the clearing banks in contempt both because there is every evidence that their specialist departments are pinching business from both professions (and in their view doing it badly) and because individual bank managers do not always understand the nuances of accounts prepared on a going-concern basis and so will not lend to their clients. (A going-concern basis demands that a business be valued on the assumption that it can keep trading, whereas a banker, from bitter experience, wants to know what he can save from the wreck when it stops.)

This brings us to the real problem. Bankers are disliked because they have money and can dispense or withhold it. Accountants generally cannot, so even if they hold the view that most bank managers can't count beyond 12 with their socks on, they have to tolerate them.

Jobs in Practice

Cobblers' children are the worst shod. The practice of management within firms of accountants differs somewhat from the practice of management in other commercial firms. Not to put too fine a point on it, management has been conspicuous by its absence.

Accountants have been trained to be accountants, not managers, and if they stay in public practice have little or no exposure to good examples of modern methods. A few key examples may help demonstrate this:

a) The 'personnel' function is usually concerned only with recruitment, to cope with the high staff turnover caused by the lack of management (or of a real personnel function). Human resources departments even fire people badly.
b) Decisions are made by committee with no one individual responsible for key areas. Hence, people tend to be against things rather than for them.
c) It is more fun doing client work than managing
d) The senior partner is either an autocrat or weak
e) Training which is unrelated to the task of extracting money from the clients is generally low priority or non-existent
f) Good practice in recruitment costs more than the old methods and is therefore to be avoided, so they keep hiring the wrong people.

These symptoms are probably at their worst in accountancy because accountancy is supposed to be a business education and some members of the profession actually believe their own propaganda to the extent that they think they know everything on the day they qualify.

Now that you appreciate the constraints, it is permissible to explore the organisation structure of a typical firm. The profession divides its staff into three categories:

1. The partners
2. The qualified or potentially qualified
3. The rest.

There are subtle distinctions within each category.

1. The Partners

There will normally be a **senior partner** who may or may not be in charge in that his authority is shared or usurped by a committee, variously known as the policy committee, management committee or wrecking crew. This is because the senior partner is either very democratic or incompetent.

Next, oddly enough, comes a **consultant** or consultants, usually ex senior partners who won't go away. This sub-group is not obligatory, but there are a lot of them around.

After this come the **full partners**, then the **junior partners** and finally the **salaried partners** who, by definition, receive a salary but do not share in the profits.

Ranking with this group, but in 'the rest' for other purposes, is an odd category found in a minority of firms – the **directors**. They are so called because they are not qualified accountants or have the 'wrong' qualification and therefore cannot be admitted to partnership. They attain director status because they have skills indispensable to the partnership and they may actually be real directors of a real associated company, typically in consultancy work. They are likely to be brighter and better rewarded than the average partner.

2. The Qualified

The next category covers all qualified employees, students and people who have abandoned their studies. There are several levels in this sub-group. In the sort of firm where they desperately need status symbols to disguise the poor pay or the lack of partnership prospects, the full range would include **senior manager**, **manager**, **assistant manager**, **senior** (clerk), **semi-senior** and of course the bright young **trainees**, described as 'students' or 'articled clerks' depending on the age of the partner describing them. Use of the latter term dates one considerably.

One major advantage of these delicate shadings is that firms can charge more per hour for each grade's services than for the one below. It is difficult to find managerially acceptable reasons for them.

3. The Rest

'The rest' may include only clerical staff in a small practice, but in a larger practice will include some non-accountants akin to the directors described above, who are there because they know things that accountants don't know fully or at all. They are usually the nucleus of a consulting practice. The profession is so ambivalent about their existence that there is no unanimity of titles.

Similarly, there is some confusion about the best of the rest, typically called 'partnership secretary' or 'administration director', who is here because the partners have decided that they cannot manage the internal affairs of the firm and have brought in a professional manager from outside to relieve them of the problem. These managers are usually retired senior officers, which tells us something about the profession's view of management.

The creation of this buffer is generally a good thing, with the exception of the case a few years ago when a distinguished London partnership hired one to curb the wilder excesses of the senior partner and to distance them from the problems he created.

Unfortunately, because accountants in practice are very discreet, neither the job description nor the interview process and induction programme gave any hint of the need to restrain the boss. It was assumed that the need for this was self-evident. In the event, the need was evident but the newcomer, as a good manager, knew that he did not have a mandate for the task, which therefore went undone. Only when the newcomer was fired for not achieving results in this area and took legal action against the partnership did the sorry story emerge.

Jobs in Commerce

The senior positions are headed by a **Financial Director**. Some very big companies have two. This is usually because the first one wasn't quite good enough but has a major shareholding or knows something he shouldn't.

The **Company Secretary** usually reports to the **Financial Director** but the two roles are separate. Only in a very small company, or a very Victorian one, will they be combined. Beware the latter. Quill pens will be in evidence. It is tolerable for the Financial Controller to be Secretary as well but if the Secretary is also Chief Accountant this is another reactionary sign.

Controllers, by the way, usually do what Chief Accountants used to do, only more so. If the company has both Chief Accountant and Controller, history probably imposed the latter over the former, who will now be sitting in a back room ticking off the days to his pension and mumbling quietly in his beard.

Do not trust accountants with beards unless they have become entrepreneurs, when you can mistrust them for entirely different reasons. The 'Hickson rules' of management selection totally exclude hiring people with beards to work as accountants. The originator of these rules was so successful at relating unacceptable personal characteristics to beards that in a controlled test in 1985 he was able to identify an accountant who had had a beard (the previous year) and one who had not yet grown a beard but did so some months later.

On the same level as the Controller you may also find a **Treasurer**, if the company has substantial money opportunities (or problems, as they used to be called) and wishes to hedge its bets about money – or about the succession to the financial directorship.

Succession in the finance function is usually pretty good. There are several reasons for this:

a) If things go badly wrong the Finance Director gets fired.
b) If things go very right as a result of the F.D.'s work he or she gets the top job or a wider commercial role.
c) Good F.Ds get headhunted.
d) Only the F.D. has a complete overview of the company's affairs and is thus a safe bet as successor if the Managing Director falls under a bus.

e) In adverse conditions, the F.D. best knows where to cut and again gets the top job if the M.D. has been profligate or is for other reasons the preferred scapegoat.
f) The Human Resource Director who in theory should know how to manage the other major resource (the people who make the money) has been brainwashed into subservience to mammon and its high priests, so does not push for the job.

All these events enable the Controller to participate in the game of musical chairs, unless the Treasurer has been coming up fast on the inside.

If you have dealings with any organisation's finance staff it is also very important to know who actually monitors and influences what goes on in the organisation as a whole, and who are merely bean-counters. Fortunately job titles tend to be reasonable indicators, except in the sort of company which is too apolitical or too small to have definitive titles.

For cases where the title doesn't help, observe the frequency with which people venture beyond the confines of the finance offices. The most regular travellers will be the real accountants.

The key job titles have changed over the years. Before and just after the war it was likely to be the 'cost accountant' who found out what the numbers meant. Then there was a brief period when the 'budget accountant' meant something, followed by a long run for 'management accountants' before the current vogue for 'financial analysts' as the sharp end of the team. Any company using the older titles is also telling you something about itself.

New wave analysts become new wave controllers. Your chances of promotion are affected not only by your merits but by your job title and in a new wave company it is vital to have a title that omits the word 'accountant'. Inventing a good title for a new job is more than half the battle.

Affiliations

Old soldiers never die, they only fade away. What happens to accountants? Many accountants stop being accountants at a relatively early age. They move into general management or into other functions.

There is also a substantial minority movement into non-managerial streams. Some go into **consultancy**, in the true sense. Some have consultancy thrust upon them, by redundancy. Some are born to consultancy in that it fits them so well they become company doctors. There are two types of company doctor:

1. Those who keep on doing it because they love it and can make a living at it.

2. Those who have nothing better to do, because they are unemployed and can take the risk.

Where else would you find someone mug enough to work for a company which is close to insolvency, with no job security and the chance that one's fees will not be paid if the results are not successful?

Others become **entrepreneurs**. The word used to be complimentary but is now applied to those whose skills or specialisation defy ready description. They may not actually be drug-runners but one is left in some doubt.

Yet others, from a base in public practice, become

the vultures of business as **liquidators** and **receivers**, although it is slightly unfair to classify the latter thus. Receivers actually run a business for a while before, with luck, returning it to normal operation whereas liquidators are likely to sell the assets, which may or may not re-emerge attached to the rest of the business (employees, trademarks, etc.).

Finally, the more sensible 'consultants' and 'company doctors' eventually become professional **non-executive directors**, usually with a portfolio of companies. This is both safer and less stressful.

Do not assume from all this that accountants want to be something else. They are generally content with, even complacent about, their choice of profession. It can lead to other things so easily. Given the mega-mergers of accountancy firms, 'other things' include unemployment.

Accountants' Skills

It is well known that 'turf accountant' is a euphemism for bookmaker. Some who should know better also suggest that 'accountant' is a euphemism for bookkeeper. This is unfair. Accountancy, *per se*, is a fairly basic expertise but the qualified accountant has to have a catholic range of skills and knowledge beyond pure accountancy.

An accountant has to be familiar with auditing, book-keeping, credit management, electronic data processing, insurance, law, management, personnel practice, company secretarial work, tax and treasury matters. Every one of these specialisations has its own 'professional' body nowadays. The accountant may be master of none but can understand what is going on in each well enough to communicate with members of each of these new professions.

Erudite accountants sometimes describe themselves as profit engineers or even polymaths, not as jacks of all trades. Alas, this broad business knowledge is allied to a somewhat parochial approach to wider matters. A good example is the accountant who in the space marked 'languages' on a job application form wrote BASIC, COBOL and FORTRAN.

There are also a number of Lesser Known Facts about accountants.

Colour prejudice. According to reliable sources in the direct mail business, accountants' favourite colour is blue. Send them an envelope with lots of blue on it and their natural resistance to junk mail is eroded.

Que? When accountants use the letter K to indicate a number they usually mean 1000, rather than the true figure of 1024. This is because most of them do not fully understand binary arithmetic. If they are Spanish of course K means 'what?'.

Equity to real people means fairness. To accountants it means share capital. Fairness only comes into the 'true and fair view' – an academic concept which auditors are required to certify on annual accounts.

Auditors are not supposed to detect fraud. The judicial view is that they are 'watchdogs, not bloodhounds'. So, much press comment about auditors failing in their duty in fraud cases is likely to be written by journalists who, as a whole, are usually chronically reluctant to research the context before venturing opinions. So are most politicians who do not see that perfect audit could cost all the corporate profit, and yet be imperfect.

Practice Development is a euphemism for marketing, used in the practising side of the profession when all forms of advertising were forbidden. The term has remained although ethical constraints have softened. The key marketing man in a practice is known as the senior drinking partner, who is unlikely to be senior partner but will be extrovert and clubbable. He may or may not be a good technical accountant but is very likely to be a good communicator, trainer and manager. For obvious reasons, senior drinking partners are not listed as such in company brochures, but it is as well to know at least one of them in the top 12 firms. Knowing two or more means you have arrived socially.

The **patron Saint** of accountants and tax gatherers is St Matthew. Most accountants don't mention the enforced union with VAT men and the Revenue.

Background

Who invented accountancy? There are several answers to this. The Koreans may have done. The Chinese did too. So did the Egyptians and the Greeks. The Romans probably plagiarised Greek precedents. The Phoenicians almost certainly had their own system.

Most of these are likely to have been separate 'inventions', which reminds us of our earlier conclusion that accountancy is very simple conceptually and thus quite easy to invent.

The other reason that it had to be reinvented,

rather than introduced from country to country, is that it is difficult to engender enthusiasm for pedestrian concepts before local need causes them to be invented locally.

However, at the eastern end of the Mediterranean, accountancy may well have travelled the camel routes. Most countries in that region had some form of accountancy before the rest of the world and in the case of the Babylonians, 2000 BC is the likely period.

Even the Assyrians, who are best remembered for their warlike qualities, had a simple form of accountancy at an early date. It may be that the historical references have been misunderstood and that when the Assyrians came down 'like a wolf on the fold' the scribe was referring to a dawn raid by a team of tax-gatherers or auditors.

International acceptance and codification had to wait a while, until the Romans put out a basic accounting system to their various dominions for the purposes of tax collection: in much the same way that ITT and IBM issue accounting manuals to their farflung offshoots today.

The Italians, although not first with the concept of accountancy can be held to have been the inventors of double-entry book-keeping. Pacioli's *Summa de Arithmetica* contained, in 1494, the first published description thereof.

The paucity of accounting in the centuries BC and the diversity of systems in the Middle Ages settled down to a more limited sample by Victorian times. Variations tended to depend on whose empire you were in, so that the British Empire had one set of rules, the French another, based on the Code Napoleon and the various German, Spanish and Portuguese territories had slightly different practices.

In the East the Japanese remained largely aloof from external influence and the Chinese knowing the world revolved around them saw no reason to change much except documents prepared exclusively for the barbarians.

The 20th century saw a new Empire, that of the American multinational companies, bringing with it the accounting requirements of the Securities Exchange Commission, SEC for short, so that even in those territories where they cling grimly to the old local ways, everything eventually gets translated into a form acceptable to the US regulatory authorities.

Most 'Western' countries have their own professional accounting bodies, often with chauvinist requirements as to eligibility (nowhere more so than in France, the birthplace of M. Chauvin). There is one major exception. The Commonwealth has an Imperial relic, in the form of overseas members of two British bodies, the Certified, and the Management accountants. Both of these have a substantial minority of overseas members, some exported from the UK but many home-grown in their countries of origin.

The Italians are still in the forefront of accountancy development. Most of the world makes do with one set of books. The French allegedly have two. The Italians have three, one for the taxman, one for the shareholders and one showing the real picture. (This last is usually kept off-site in a remote mountain fastness.)

The Greeks are even craftier. They have one set for the government and a second for their accountants. The third set is for themselves – concealed from the accountants, who would otherwise be rewarded by the government with a 10 per cent commission on the fiddles discovered.

THE AUTHOR

John Courtis is a Chartered Accountant.

His experience of accountancy gained in public practice, the Royal Air Force and Ford Motor Company led him to leave accounting behind over twenty years ago. He is now a headhunter as senior partner of John Courtis & Partners and a full member of the Institute of Personnel & Development, but assures us he is no more a personnel manager than he is an accountant.

He is also active in training, management education and freelance journalism, having written for numerous magazines, most of which are now defunct. Ten of his twenty published books are still in print, i.e. selling quite slowly.

He owns a number of odd cars and eccentric cameras, has absolutely no sporting interests and dislikes most indoor games except those he can win. These include Trivial Pursuits, liar dice and draughts.